Praise for

La Musica...

"Giovanni Gaudelli is affectionately known by me and many others as 'Giomotivation.' He is a master communicator. He has become a stalwart source of encouragement and inspiration in my life. He writes this masterpiece of practical living instructions to help you and I become our own musical conductor and "maestro." I recommend wholeheartedly that you read Gio's book to gain insight on how to get more fulfillment and satisfaction from your life and career. You will have to read it to figure out how being a slush buster and a back washer can help you do this, and improve your performance . . . but then, that will be just one of the pleasant surprises you gain from reading Gio's La Musica."

-Timothy Grant Carter, a.k.a. "Slam," Professional Speaker, and Author of the Best Selling Book, *Positive x Positive = Unlimited*, Thomasville, North Carolina, USA

"I have always been inspired by Giovanni Gaudelli through his posts on social media, but to now have an entire book with his wisdom and inspiration is absolutely amazing. The book makes me really think about life and how I am tapping into my personal greatness. The book is a must-read for anyone who is looking to grow personally or professionally."

-Cynthia Bazin, President of SmartChic (www.smartchic.me) and Sacramento City Editor of Today's Innovative Woman, California, USA

"Dynamic, enthusiastic, sincere, and humorous! I've been associated with Giovanni for the better part of four decades. Those adjectives aptly describe the author. No matter your field of discipline, if you are committed to taking your game to the next level, this book is a compelling guide."

-Robert A. Mariani, Chartered Life Underwriter and Financial Security Advisor, Pointe-Claire, Canada

"The whole book is inspiring. What has really touched me is one of the last chapters, "La Musica." I have always considered our hotel as a theatre, where guests are spectators, staff members are actors, and I am the "maestro," the director. The play changes every day, but the constant thread is "La Musica." It flows from the leader through the staff, entertaining the guests and making their stay a memorable experience. Read the book, and let your "Musica" play!"

-Alfonso Imperato, Director, Pietra di Luna Hotel, Maiori, Italy

"Giovanni Gaudelli is a powerful and engaging keynote speaker who speaks to us in terms we can all understand and relate to. In this wonderful and inspiring book, Giovanni shares his understanding of what makes us tick. The book is upbeat, encouraging, and full of memorable anecdotes. Not only will you learn how to get in tune with your own inner musica, but his passion and zest for life are contagious and will help you find deeper meaning and authenticity in your life."

-Richard Flowers, Chief Executive Officer, Social Security Board, Belize

"I highly recommend reading Giovanni's book. Giovanni illustrates the tremendous ability that each of us has within us to achieve personal excellence. He demonstrates the power of attitude through impactful stories and analogies. He reminds us that WE control how we respond to adversity and that WE can create positive outcomes in life. Giovanni will inspire and challenge you to be your personal best!"

-Lisa Hoy Pressick, Sales Leader,
State Farm Insurance Companies, Ajax East, Canada

"Have you found your MUSICA? I first heard about Giovanni Gaudelli's amazing concept a few years ago when I shared the stage with him at a speaking event. I discovered an exceptional speaker and a man with a big heart. This book is a lot like Giovanni. It's full of beautiful inspiring MUSICA. It offers a delightful and refreshing approach that you can apply to all aspects of your life. It will open your heart to your own wonderful MUSICA. This book is a gift. It is stimulating, invigorating, and energizing. Read it and you will feel an irresistible drive to bring out the best in yourself and others."

-Sylvain Guimond, Ph.D., Sport Psychology Specialist, International Consultant to World-Class Athletes, Author, Speaker, and Founding President of Biotonix, Sorel, Canada

La Musica

Also by Splendor Publishing

Positive x Positive = Unlimited
High Octane Positive Energy

The Art & Science of Loving Yourself First
'cause Your Business Should Complete You Not Deplete You!

25 Brilliant Business Mentors
Their Top Tips to Catapult You to Success

25 Brilliant Speakers
Their Expert Advice to Springboard
Your Speaking Career

The Happy Law Practice
Expert Strategies to Build Business
While Maintaining Peace of Mind

Winning Ways in Commercial Real Estate
18 Successful Women Unveil the Tips of the Trade
in the Real Estate World

The Substance of Faith
Get Hooked—It's Good Stuff!

La Musica

ARE YOU PLAYING YOUR SONG?

RELEASE THE MAESTRO WITHIN YOU

GIOVANNI GAUDELLI

Splendor Publishing
College Station, TX

SPLENDOR PUBLISHING
Published by Splendor Publishing,
College Station, TX.

First published printing in the English language, May, 2015

La Musica—Are You Playing Your Song? is an expanded and revised version of the book originally published in French under the title *"La Musica Au coeur de chaque leader"* in 2013 by Éditions Giomotivation. Original publication ISBN 978-2-98141-050-4.

The author and publisher have made every effort to include accurate information and website addresses in this work at the time of publication, and assume no responsibility for changes, omissions, inaccuracies, or errors that occur before or after publication.

Library of Congress Control Number: 2015938820
La Musica—Are You Playing Your Song?

ISBN-10:1-940278-10-4   ISBN-13:978-1-940278-10-0
Business/Self Help

Printed in the United States of America.

Interior photos and illustrations: ©istock.com

Cover art: © Abimages | Dreamstime.com, © Angelp Vectorstock.com
La Musica Man art, page 100: © Florianr | Dreamstime.com

For more information or to order bulk copies of this book for events, seminars, conferences, or training, contact SplendorPublishing.com.

Dedication

I dedicate this book to my parents,
Agostino Gaudelli and Viviana Meola. They were
my first leaders. Their dedication, caring, love, and
determination have been a great example for me.
Even though they are no longer of this world,
they are still with me as my guardian angels.

" **We** all have the extraordinary coded within us, waiting to be released. "

— Jean Houston

Contents

FOREWORD

Who is Giovanni Gaudelli, also known as Gio? I discovered Giovanni in 2003 during a major leadership conference held in Montreal, Canada. First impression? With his accent and his unique Italian style, he reminded me of the famous actor Danny DeVito. I laughed so hard, I was in tears. But I soon realized that this outstanding speaker was more than a comedian. He was the real deal! Young at heart and with remarkable authenticity, Giovanni demonstrated an impressive understanding of human behavior.

Since 2003, I've had the privilege of attending Giovanni's presentations more than a dozen times, as I got him invited to speak to various employee training events. Every time, I came out with a better understanding of what we can do to live a genuinely happy life and attain professional success.

Whether it's to improve teamwork, enhance management and leadership abilities, assist sales teams with their results, help public sector employees deliver excellent service, or to encourage people to be their very best, Giovanni's message is relevant and powerful. What he teaches with so much pizzazz is in fact very simple: we must be willing to listen to the MUSICA which emanates from deep inside ourselves and our surroundings. As soon as we're "off-key," we need to look immediately beyond our behavior and examine attentively our attitudes, beliefs, values, and what Giovanni calls our programming. To illustrate his ideas and anchor them in the reality of everyday life, Giovanni draws his inspiration from his own experiences as a teacher, father, and business owner.

The teachings and life lessons shared by Giovanni Gaudelli in this book are bound to move you deeply. Thanks to Giovanni, I have substantially improved the quality of my own professional and family life. Dear reader, I sincerely wish that this book will do the same for you. This is a wonderful opportunity for you to open up to new empowering perspectives and to add your own unique voice to a positive and uplifting chorus line: Viva la MUSICA!

Richard Rochefort
Former Assistant Deputy Minister,
Government of Canada

Acknowledgements

I want to thank Margo DeGange for her amazing support and for helping me bring this book to the world. I also want to express my gratitude to the team of editors at Splendor Publishing. A very special thank you also goes to Jacqueline Snider, my personal editor, who from the onset assisted me in writing and editing my book.

I am thankful for the support of Nicole Bronsard, Michel Bélanger, Claude Janet, Florence Buathier, and Brigittte Ayotte who helped me bring forth the original French publication of this book in 2013. Their assistance and belief in the value of my message has prompted me to create this English version.

I also want to thank all those who I have had the pleasure to work with—clients, colleagues, managers, coaches, or consultants. I have learned so much from these experiences and interactions and I am ever so thankful. In particular, I want to thank Robert Mariani, my mentor, whose leadership has been a constant inspiration to me.

I am deeply grateful for the love and support of my wife Manon and our two children, Sabrina and Adamo, who have always believed in me and continue to share with me their tremendous "musica" which gives me so much energy to keep going further.

To those of you who will be reading this book, I thank you and hope that I will contribute to the achievement of your objectives.

May magnificence fill your days!

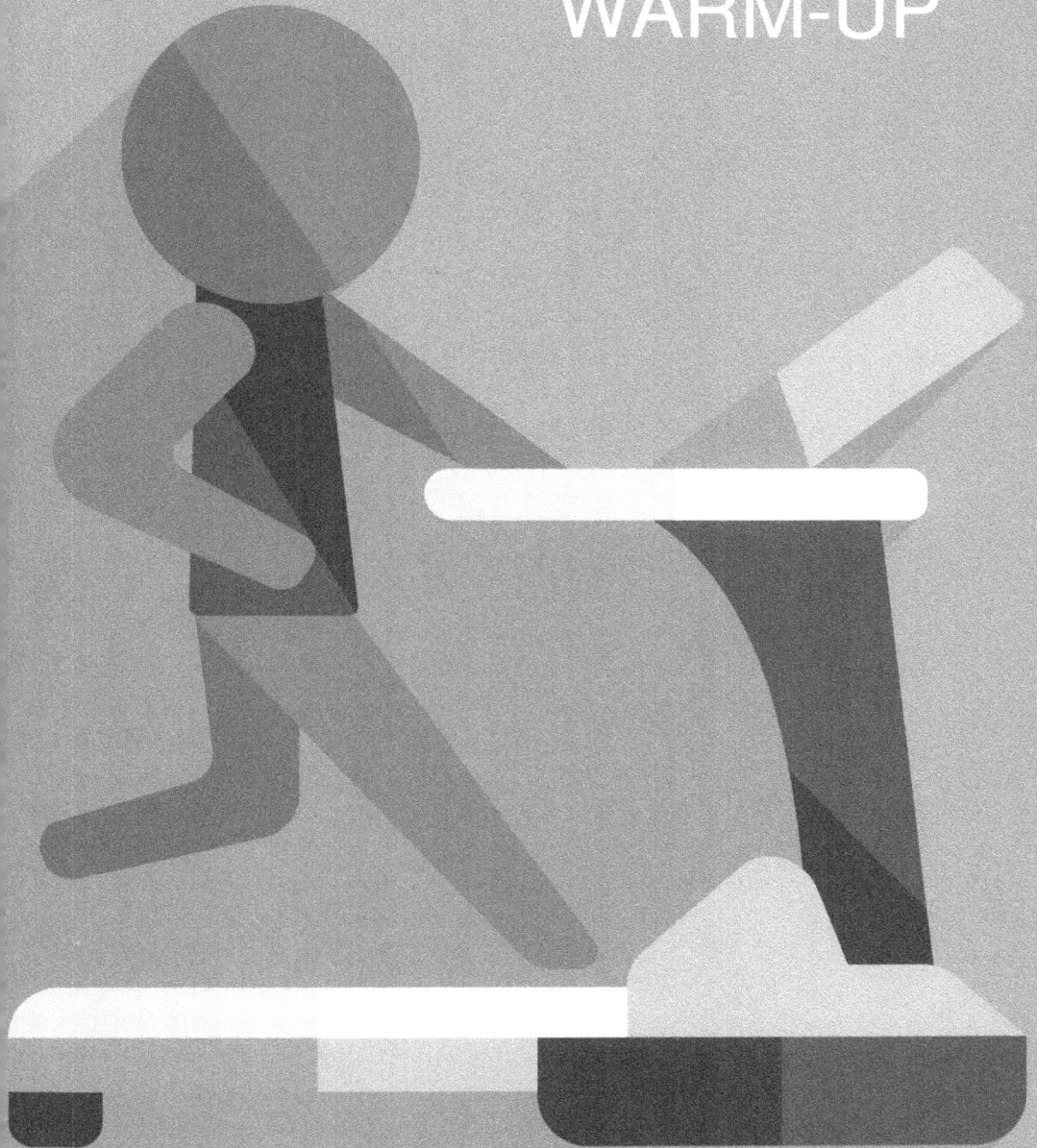

Introduction

THE WARM-UP

"**D**o not go where the path may lead, go instead where there is no path and leave a trail."

-Ralph Waldo Emerson

♪ ♫

The Warm-Up

How it All Began

I've been delivering motivational and keynote messages for more than 15 years. I've often been moved by the spontaneous and positive feedback people have shared with me after my presentations. Many heart-warming testimonials and constant requests for electronic or print copies of my presentations have led me to believe that there's a need for a "portable" Giovanni. This is how I became inspired to write this book.

I graduated from McGill University in 1976 with a Bachelor of Arts in English Literature and Italian as a second language. I went on to graduate school to get my teaching diploma, which I received in June 1977. I then worked as a teacher, teaching English as a second language to what were considered very difficult high school students. My parents, who emigrated from Italy in the 1950s, were extremely proud of their Giovanni who had gone to university and became a "professor."

In 1980, I changed careers and joined the London Life Insurance Company to be a life insurance agent. I was still quite young at the time and was willing to take the risk. In the worst case scenario, I could always return to teaching if my venture proved to be unsuccessful. I remained in the financial services industry for 30 years until I sold my practice to devote all my time to my speaking engagements, consulting, and coaching. During those 30 years, I spent 26 years hiring, training, leading, and coaching hundreds of young inexperienced and older experienced men and women.

Now why would I want to publish a self-help book considering the astounding number of best sellers already available on the market? The answer is simple: from those years, I want to share with you all that I have learned and experienced about this wonderful being, the "human" being. My objective is to impart to you what I believe is the most essential aspect of human behavior and empower you to be the best you can be and in turn empower others. I want to share the important life lessons I've learned, not only as a business executive and motivational speaker, but as a human being working from within to inspire and motivate people. I want you to find your inner music, which I like to refer to as your "musica" in honor of my Italian origins. I want you to get in touch with your own inner leader. I want you to be your own musical conductor, your own "maestro." I want you to be the lead singer of your inner life! This is why I wrote *La Musica—Are You Playing Your Song?*

Lesson Learned

Both in the school system and business sector, I learned that the approach to training is similar. Traditionally, we train people on competencies and feed them knowledge assuming that this is what will make them achieve the desired results. Of course with all the training, come binders on top of binders, workbooks on top of workbooks, which all end up in some drawer somewhere or on some shelf collecting dust. Thus all this wonderful material that is supposed to enhance performance remains dormant in each individual's mental hard drive.

Among the many courses I followed when I was in the financial services industry, one was on excellence. Of course, that came with a binder. One late afternoon, while discussing some of the daily issues with my administrative manager, I noticed she had placed the binder on one of her shelves. I had taken the course in French and the title on the binder read "Atteindre l'excellence," which in English means "Achieving Excellence." I had an immediate flash. I realized that with all these courses and binders, even though everyone would like to "atteindre" (achieve) excellence, the vast majority end up "attendre" (waiting for) excellence. The only difference in spelling between "atteindre" and "attendre" is one letter, the letter "I."

"There it is" I told myself! The source of greatness as well as the most important ingredient to achieving anything in life is in the "I." In other words, it's ME. Being trilingual, this moment of awareness was particularly powerful since the "I" is also in the Italian "Io" and the French "Moi," two words that translate as "I" and "ME."

Each individual with its dreams, desires, fears, emotions, ambitions, or prejudices is the real show maker or show-stopper. Why do we have recessions? Why are there still wars? Why do our political leaders make the decisions they make? Why do we have so much sensationalism in the media? The answer to all these questions lies in the needs that each individual involved—each "I"—has. There is enough knowledge and software to avoid recessions. However, it's a human being that makes the final decisions. Maybe their bonus will be lower if they don't achieve a certain level of sales or stock price. Maybe they'll lose votes if they make that decision even though it might be the right one. Maybe they won't get the ratings if they don't exaggerate the news and scandals. Maybe a war away from home is economically viable. Maybe I don't even know why I'm at war; it's just the way it's always been.

My point here is not to render judgment. It is however to expose without a shadow of a doubt that to affect change, performance, improvements, peace of mind, enthusiasm, health, or happiness, we need to positively and intensely influence the source of it all, the "I."

Empowering the "I"

I believe that one of the most important aspects of a self-help book is its ability to inspire people to take action. My experience tells me that when you approach people with logic, tell them what to do and how to do it, you might get some temporary action out of them, but in the end, chances are, old ingrained problematic behaviors or attitudes will keep the upper hand.

This is why *La Musica—Are You Playing Your Song?* presents information and ideas in such a way as to create positive emotional experiences within the reader, which in turn creates a desire to change. The book is empowering and transformative and the reader will particularly appreciate:

♪ Its ability to touch the inner "I" across generations, gender, culture, and language;

♪ Its capacity to bypass the logical mind in order to reach the core emotional heart of the reader;

♪ Its simple, down-to-earth ideas and stories that produce compelling experiences and emotions;

♪ Its understanding of what makes people "tick," so they can spontaneously embrace more fulfilling behaviors;

♪ Its easy-to-grasp concept that includes a step-by-step diagram illustrating how our beliefs influence our attitudes, emotions, actions, and ultimately our results; and

♪ Its joyful and passionate approach to inner work.

Tiramisù for the Soul

While there are many amazing self-help books on the market, many of which have brilliantly survived the passage of time, I believe that every author who has ever published has brought his or her own unique flavor to the world. My table is set to offer a taste of tiramisù, a popular coffee-flavored Italian dessert, which literally means *Pull Me Up*!

Inspiring transformation in people and inciting them to take action is one of the most rewarding aspects of my activities as a motivational speaker and coach. Over and over again and to my great satisfaction, I've listened to people tell me how much my message "sticks" with them. This is what the book is all about: creating awareness, enhancing consciousness, touching core beliefs to foster lasting change, and opening up the reader to a creative and joyous life.

It's a fresh and experiential approach to the forces at work within us. *La Musica—Are You Playing Your Song?* helps readers experience the full circle of human activity, from behaviors to emotions, from attitudes to beliefs, empowering them every step of the way to take hold of their lives. It's an open conversation between the author and the reader, an invitation for everyone to find their own beat, turn on their light, and let their "musica" be heard.

So hang on for a special ride as I take us on a journey of exploration, revelation, and empowerment. I invite you to give yourself the gift of time; time for reflection and time to get in touch with the amazing person you really are. I encourage you to listen to the "musica" within, "compose," and write down your own notes throughout the book.

May your journey be "magnifico"!

❧❧

Chapter 1

WALKING OUR TALK

" *A leader is great, not because of his or her power, but because of his or her ability to empower others.* "

-John C. Maxwell

♪ ♫
Walking Our Talk

We are ALL Leaders

I know we've all heard of "walking our talk" before; however, how many of us really do it? It's almost as if we expect it from others, but not from ourselves. So if we take this to its logical limit, nobody will do it. I want us to accept that we are ALL leaders from the day we are born. All of us in our own very special ways know how to lead ourselves and have led others. If you think about it, when we are just about to take our first steps to walk, aren't we demonstrating leadership? We are showing our determination to our parents, feeling a tremendous boost of energy from this accomplishment, and creating a desire to go further.

When we're in school as early as kindergarten, we are learning to share with others, learning how to read, how to respect deadlines, and how to be on time. Some kids can even help their parents find their way around the latest devices and technology. Isn't that leadership? When I say everyone is a leader, it really means there is a leader in each of us.

When my parents emigrated from Italy, they arrived here with literally what they were wearing and a suitcase filled with personal belongings. They had no jobs and no titles, but a huge belief that they were going to make it work. My mother worked in a clothing factory as a seamstress and in quality control. My father worked for what was, at the time, the largest retail store in the country, Eaton's. It was Canada's Macy's. He worked as a warehouse foreman. No car, no subway, but come hell or high water they pushed themselves every day towards their dream of raising a family where there was always food on the table, shelter, love, discipline, and access to education. Looks like leadership by example to me. They walked their talk.

There are millions of examples like my parents in North America and we can all learn from their tremendous leadership.

Unfortunately, as we grow up in a society where there seems to have to be a "logical" explanation for everything, leadership seems to be only for those who have a "leadership title" next to their name. Leaders and followers are a bit like the "chicken and the egg" situation. Leaders with no followers are leading no one and all leaders also need to be followers or they will not grow. So we are ALL leaders and followers. We cannot control who will follow us. We can only control who we will follow and how we will lead our lives. If we ALL accept that there is a leader inside all of us and let that propel us to being our best, automatically we will have followers and we will ALL be moving forward.

That, I believe, is the first step to walking our talk. This is what makes us take responsibility for our actions. This is what shows authenticity. This is what gives others the energy,

NOTES _____

_____

_____

courage, and desire to also walk their talk. This shows leadership and conviction.

Look at our politicians. How many walk their talk? They're so caught up with getting votes that they are trying to walk everyone else's talk. I don't think I need to tell you what the results are, do I? It's been said that you cannot please everyone, and when you try, you usually end up pleasing no one.

As a result, we have created an environment where we constantly look to put the blame anywhere but on ourselves. And yet, the only control we have is on our "I."

Looking Within

If there is an issue with our car, our computer, our stove, our lawn mower, or our phone, we immediately take action to get them fixed so they get back to being 100 percent functional.

Our "I" is the most important ingredient in whatever we want to achieve in our lives, but when our "I" is not at 100 percent, how long do we wait before fixing it? The first step to fixing our "I" is to walk our talk. If we do not take this first essential step, then we are setting ourselves up to be "walked" by other people's talk and feeling unfulfilled in our own objectives.

Whenever there is an issue or a problem in achieving results, we tend to always look for the cause and solution by pointing a finger outside of ourselves. We're constantly

NOTES _____

_____

_____

looking to point out as opposed to pointing in. We have a tendency to cast blame outside of our responsibility, looking for solutions from "without" as opposed to "within." Yet, the best solutions lie "within" and are 100 percent controllable, while on the other hand, we cannot control what's happening "without."

What Really Matters

In this age of technology, we all work with a computer. When our computer has a bug, we immediately want to fix it and we start the process of repairing it right away. Our computer is extremely essential for achieving our results, and when it is not performing at its best, we immediately want to bring it back to 100 percent. So we re-boot, side-boot, under-boot, over-boot, kick-boot, and ultimately call for help!

However, when our "I" has a bug, we do not immediately begin the process of fixing it even though it's our most important ingredient. Instead, we prefer to complain and vent our frustrations. There are two unwritten rules about complaining:

1. We must find someone else to complain with, and

2. The other person listening will be thinking of an even bigger complaint than ours and will be more than eager to share it.

It doesn't take long for our initial "bug" to get bigger and

NOTES _____

_____

_____

worse. We are feeling far from our 100 percent and we haven't even started working on fixing the bug yet. As a result, we will behave in a way that will likely not help us attain the results we were hoping for.

I want us to walk our talk by accepting that our "I" is the most important ingredient in achieving our results. We must begin the process of fixing our "bug" immediately, just as we would for our computer.

This action alone will have amazing results. Just as a musical instrument whose chords are out of tune, when our "I" is performing at 60 percent, 50 percent, or even less, it will have a tremendous negative impact on our results. However, when our "I" is performing at 100 percent, it will automatically have a tremendous positive impact on all aspects of our lives.

Think of just *one* specific action you can take immediately where you will be "walking your talk" in at least one aspect of your life. The positive effects of walking this talk will be tremendous.

NOTES

NOTES

Chapter 2

THE DO-RE-ME CIRCLE

"You must be the change you wish to see in the world.

—Mahatma Gandhi

♪ ♫
The DO-RE-ME Circle

The Cycle of Human Behavior

Human behavior is like a cycle. It can be a positive, invigorating, vivacious cycle, but it can also be a negative, depressing, vicious cycle as we spin our wheels from one negative cycle to another. The longer we remain in the positive vivacious cycle the better results we see, and of course vice versa. Unfortunately, we are generally not aware of our behaviors.

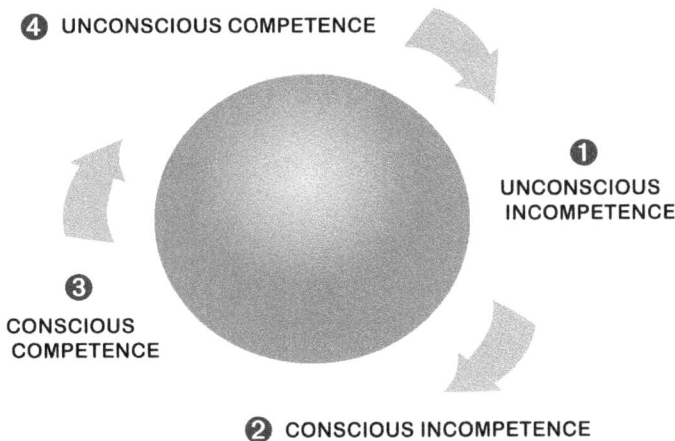

4 UNCONSCIOUS COMPETENCE

1 UNCONSCIOUS INCOMPETENCE

3 CONSCIOUS COMPETENCE

2 CONSCIOUS INCOMPETENCE

Competence Cycle

There are four states of behavior:

1. Unconscious incompetence
2. Conscious incompetence
3. Conscious competence
4. Unconscious competence

Moving to the Conscious Modes

Our goal is to go from the first state to the fourth. When we are unconsciously incompetent or unconsciously competent we are relaxed, confident, and comfortable. We are in our "comfort zone." Even though we may not be competent, we are unconscious of it. To change or improve our behavior, we must move to the conscious modes. The first conscious mode is conscious incompetence, where we realize and accept we need to improve. We know that we have a "bug" and begin to consciously fix it. We then move on to conscious competence, where we discover and learn a new model. It is during this conscious state that we reflect on our decisions to create our desired results.

It's a challenge to remain in this conscious state. We are uncomfortable here and our reflex is to go back to where we were because it feels comfortable and familiar. The objective is to remain in this conscious state long enough to

NOTES

20

repeat the new behavior. It will ultimately become our NEW unconscious competent state, where we will be better and also comfortable.

All new jobs, projects, and goals will put us through this series of states. Ideally, we should be able to enter these states without the need of a new job or project. However, our brain loves the unconscious states and will challenge us to go back there because it feels so familiar. This is why old habits are so hard to break. It takes continual conscious effort to affect change or improvement and create new lasting behaviors and results in our lives.

Something as simple as brushing our teeth, which we can perform with our eyes closed, is total unconscious competence. At some point however when we were children, it required continued conscious effort on our part—even help from our parents—before it became comfortable and easy to do.

A Continuous Process

Why is it when we start a new job or new relationship we are so "gung ho" and enthusiastic? We refer to it as the "honeymoon" period. We are moving from the conscious incompetent state to the conscious competent one. In other words, we have moved from the state of being conscious of what we needed to learn and do, to a state of knowing and doing what we need to do to get the desired results. As long as we stay in this conscious competent state, we will be enthusiastic and we will continue to grow and succeed.

NOTES

However, as we become good at something, we move to the unconscious competent state as illustrated by the Competence Cycle. It's comfortable, fun, and doesn't feel like a lot of effort. It's become a reflex. The longer we allow ourselves to stay in this state instead of moving back into one of the two conscious states, the higher the likelihood and probably the certainty, that we will become unconsciously incompetent again.

Please understand that incompetence and competence are terms used to signify regression (incompetence) or improvement (competence) and not necessarily absolute competence or incompetence. We will never be totally competent or incompetent at anything. Life is an ongoing process for better or for worse depending on our choices. We will never "arrive" at ultimate competence nor will we ever be totally incompetent.

We need to allow ourselves the realization that there is room for improvement (conscious incompetence) and look for ways to improve (conscious competence). As I mentioned before, although this is preferable, it is uncomfortable because we need to make a CONSTANT conscious effort to remain here and not fall back into our comfortable (unconscious) states. This is one of the main reasons why CHANGE is so often a challenge in corporations. It's not that the change isn't good or needed or in some cases urgent, it's that human beings prefer to feel comfortable and change makes them feel uncomfortable. What's really interesting is that when there is no change, human beings will complain they're bored.

NOTES

22

So what does all this mean? It means that the real issue is not CHANGE, but instead our attitude towards change. Companies are realizing that logic alone is not enough to get employees to accept change. There needs to be actions that will impact employee attitude, as it is attitude that impacts people's emotions and ultimately their actions.

The DO-RE-ME Circle

It is for this reason that I developed the DO-RE-ME Circle. I call it DO-RE-ME for two reasons. The first reason is that it has a connection with the "musica," the music in each of us. The second reason is that it all revolves around ME, the "I." When we can understand why we are who we are and what makes us feel the way we do, we then automatically have a much better understanding of how to achieve our

NOTES

objectives and how to help others achieve theirs as well.

When we are in our unconscious states, our mental hard drive with all its knowledge is in PAUSE mode. We act as if all this knowledge doesn't exist. Our inner "musica" is off-key and becomes distorted. My intention through my DO-RE-ME Circle is to push you into the conscious states. To put your mental hard drive on PLAY, releasing all that tremendous knowledge and ability so you can achieve the results YOU want.

So let's get started!

NOTES

Chapter 3

OUT WITH LOGIC

$$M(x) = \sum_{i=1}^{n} x_i p_i$$

$$=k) = C^k \qquad p)^n$$

*" **It** is the set of the sails,
not the direction of the wind
that determines which way we
will go. "*

— Jim Rohn

♪ 𝄞

Out with Logic

FEELINGS
EMOTIONS

ACTIONS
BEHAVIOURS

RESULTS
OUTCOMES

Getting Results

Whatever results we wish for ourselves are dictated by what we will or will not do. We'll refer to these as our actions or behaviors, which are the first two steps in the DO-RE-ME Circle. This is straightforward. We must do something if we want something to be done. If we don't start anything, we can't expect anything to happen or evolve. It's a bit like a lottery. We would all like to win the jackpot, at least win something. We talk about it with our friends and confess that we are never lucky at any kind of lottery. We feel discouraged and therefore never buy tickets. In this case, what we know for sure is that we have absolutely no chances of winning. Quite simple: if we don't try anything, we won't get anything.

Pretty logical, wouldn't you say? Our actions will dictate our results. However, what dictates our actions are our *emotions*, which represents the third step in our cycle. How we *feel* about an action at the time we are about to do it will dictate whether we do it or not, and how well we do it.

We are Creatures of Emotions

How we feel is not logical, because our emotions are not logical. We don't all feel the same way about the same things and thus we don't all behave the same way, and therefore don't end up with the same *results*. We are all fundamentally creatures of emotions and not creatures of logic. If we were creatures of logic, we would all behave in the same, logical manner. And we definitely don't. This is very important because when it comes to human behavior, yours obviously included, I'm asking you to set logic aside.

I know this can be a huge challenge, especially in our North American society where everything needs to be scientific and proven. From our first day in school, we were bombarded by a logical approach to everything. That's okay for most things, but when it comes to human behavior, it just doesn't work. That's the reason why we have such a challenge understanding our behaviors. It's because we're

NOTES

always trying to understand our behaviors from a logical point of view. We must STOP!

Stopping this "logical" approach will bring your stress levels down and allow you to get on the path of affecting your behaviors. Of course, there are reasons for our behaviors but the reasons do not reside in logic. They reside in what is creating our emotions, which can be a million different things to a million different people.

Why are there so many couples today that can't find a way to get along? Why is raising a child such a challenge? Why do people feel like a failure if their boyfriend or girlfriend breaks up with them? How come my son isn't changing his behavior even though, after many discussions, he said he would? Why am I having such a hard time affecting a behavior change in one of my employees?

Stressed-out by Logic

If we use the logical approach, all these situations will continue to cause us stress and worse of all won't be resolved. We have been trained in school to learn subject matter and then pass an exam. What happens once the exam is over? Usually nothing much, we usually forget what we learned unless it's absolutely necessary for something we're doing. The brain has been trained to pass a test and then move on to other things. For example, when talking about a behavior change with our teenage son or daughter we will sit down and have a logical discussion. Our objective

NOTES

is, through logic, to get agreement and affect change. Well, what happens three days after the discussion when our son promised to change? We're back at square one, our logical thinking doesn't understand why it didn't work, and our stress level goes up.

Too many times, this just repeats itself until we lose hope and quit. No change has occurred and we have put ourselves through all that stress. Not a good idea. You see, when we have that type of logical discussion with our son and he says, *"Dad, you're right, from now on . . . "* what he's really saying is *"Dad, shut up."* Of course, he wouldn't say it because we would not accept it. All our son wants to do is "pass the exam" and get on with his life. That's why he says he agrees but immediately after, goes back to his old "unconscious" comfortable state where no change occurs.

The more he does this, the more we get stressed because it's not logical. Remember, he's not logical, he's human. Instead try this. Next time a similar situation occurs and he says, *"Dad, you're right,"* acknowledge his intent but finish off like this: *"Son, I'm really glad we agree, I will ask you for a small favor."* At this point your son will say *"Okay, Dad"* since he wants to just "pass the test." Now ask him for one specific action that he will begin doing right away to start changing his behavior. You will immediately notice a change in his facial expression as he now must actually think of something, which wasn't in his plans to "pass the test." Now, he must think of a specific action. He has moved into a conscious incompetence state and is on the

NOTES

way to conscious competence, which is totally uncomfortable. However, the chances of improvement are substantially higher. The great factor here is that if he doesn't perform his specific task, we are not as stressed out, since we are not in logical mode. The only thing we have to manage is a specific task and not ALL of his behavior.

Remember that there are always side effects to actions. Once your son starts getting used to performing his new task properly, other positive side effects will happen effortlessly. Also, by focusing on a specific behavior we avoid saying things like, *"You're so lazy"* or *"You're never on time"* or *"You're so sloppy."* These types of statements occur when we're in logical mode, which causes our stress level to increase to the point where we lose all hope and might say things that we will regret later, on top of creating a lasting negative impact.

Moving Out of the Logical Trap

What I want to achieve in this chapter is for you to let go of logic and open up to other reasons, the real ones, for behaviors. Let's say, for example, that you are in a managerial role and that you would like a behavioral change in one of your team members. First, ask yourself this question: is he behaving like this on purpose? Probably not. Next ask yourself this question: do I believe that he is capable of changing? You see if you don't "truly" believe he can change, then trust me, you will behave (unconsciously) in a way that will support your belief.

NOTES

It is extremely rare that an employee will purposely (consciously) behave in a fashion contrary to what is expected of him. Remember, we are not logical in our behaviors. That's why great managers, coaches, teachers, and parents are rare. The great ones know how to touch that emotion in us to get the desired results and don't fall into the logic trap. I am sure that all of you have had that special teacher or coach that was able to get the best out of you. They had one thing in common. Instead of relying on logic, they believed in you. They did not focus only on knowledge to help you learn. It was their ability to affect your emotions that made all the difference.

Why don't the statistically proven risks of getting lung cancer stop teens from starting to smoke? What about the danger of drinking and driving, or texting and driving, or something as simple as using your turn-signal lights when driving? We are all aware of these realities, but we don't all follow them and learn from them. Logically we should all do the right things. But we are not logical.

Look at the advertising industry. I believe that's the industry that understands human behavior the best. After all, their objective is to make us buy something whether we need it or not and to buy one brand over another. Great commercials and advertisements don't get caught up in the logical trap.

Are Buffalo jeans really sexier on us than Levi's? Are Michelin tires better than big store brands? Is Chanel really better than Christian Dior? The packaging and marketing of

NOTES _____

_____

_____

32

cosmetics costs at least ten times more than the actual product does. Gucci or Armani? Nike or Adidas? Mercedes or BMW? Lincoln or Jaguar? Cartier or Rolex? The bottom line, as my DO-RE-ME Circle suggests, is that advertisers want to create a feeling or emotion in us that makes us want to buy their product without a logical explanation as to why.

The more a product is advertised, the more it will cost us and chances are the more it will sell. Why would any company pay millions of dollars to a "star" or athlete to represent them? It's simple. It's because of how we will FEEL about their products once that star is associated with them. There is no scientific value added to a product based on who's representing it. However, there is scientific proof that the star representing the product will add to sales because of how we FEEL. Here's the doozy: we actually finance the advertising industry to convince us to buy a certain product, since the money paid to stars to represent a product is in the price paid by the consumer for the product.

I am sure you can think of many examples where the power of emotions always has the upper hand. I encourage you to become more conscious of your emotions and thoughts as this will help you pull back from the tendency to fall into the logical trap. Just think about one of your favorite songs, one that really moves you. Does it strike an emotional or a logical chord?

So out with logic and let's continue with the DO-RE-ME Circle.

NOTES

NOTES

Chapter 4

BE A
SLUSH
BUSTER

"You must weed your mind as you would weed your garden."

-Terri Guillemets

♪ ♫

Be a Slush Buster

FEELINGS
EMOTIONS

ACTIONS
BEHAVIOURS

RESULTS
OUTCOMES

Learning to Let Go

In Chapter 3, we saw through my **DO RE ME Circle** that our life results are influenced by our behaviors. We are not only creatures of action; we are also creatures of emotions and our emotions influence both our life outcomes and behaviors. We learned that our emotions have almost no basis in logic. A logical approach works for many things in our society, but it doesn't work for human behaviors and interactions.

We must learn to let go of our logical training. The approach we've been bombarded by since our childhood needs to be replaced. This is certainly a challenge, but a manageable one, I assure you!

So how do our emotions work and how do they influence our life results and behaviors? I will give you an example. What about the act of falling in love? Just the sound of it implies it's almost an accident, maybe even unconscious. We "fall for someone," it sounds unplanned and spontaneous and it often seems as if our emotions are that way. When we hire new employees for our team or decide that we want to learn to drive, we know there are logical, step-by-step criteria that we have to follow to hire that right person or pass that driver's test. But when we are looking for a mate, someone we hope to spend the rest of our lives with, 75 to 80 percent of our choice is based on our unconscious, illogical emotions.

At this point you may be asking yourself, "*How can I negate my emotions, or should I even try?*" Emotions come to the surface without warning. So, what are we supposed to do with them? How can we not feel nervous, fearful, or anxious when we actually are? And how can we feel calm when we are angry?

Becoming a Slush Buster

First of all, there are no right or wrong emotions. There are only more appropriate emotions at any particular time depending on the results we would like to achieve. Understanding the influence our emotions have on our actions helps us decide which emotion is appropriate for the situation we are in. But if we remain in an unconscious

NOTES

state, we won't be able to choose the appropriate emotion. How can we become conscious of our emotions and choose our behaviors? By becoming Slush Busters!

Here's a story that illustrates how you can become a Slush Buster in your own life. You've applied for a promotion and it's a great position. You really want to get the job. While you're waiting to hear if you'll get the interview, you may feel anxious, excited, motivated, or even uncertain. Your superior finally asks to meet with you concerning the position. What emotions do you feel at this point—nervousness, excitement, anxiety, fear? Only you know for sure. Everyone is different, and remember emotions aren't logical.

During the meeting, you find out there was a large number of applicants. Again how does this make you feel? Maybe you feel intimidated, unworthy, competitive, or confident. Again, only you know how you feel, but we all know that depending on how you feel, your behavior will change.

Your superior then announces that you're the chosen one. You feel "WOW," along with elation, happiness, joy and accomplishment. All these emotions show in your behavior and everyone around you can feel them too.

Monday comes and you're still feeling WOW. It's the beginning of spring and there's slush all over the roads, but you don't care because you're still feeling WOW. While crossing the street to your new job, your brain gives you a mini-alert: be careful, don't get splashed. Your WOW is still with you, but once you're almost across the street your brain notices a speeding car. The alert becomes more intense

NOTES _____

_____

_____

and as such your WOW is slightly less present than before. You're becoming a bit nervous.

Once you're across the street, you run into a colleague and share the details of your new promotion. He is delighted for you and is about to shake your hand to congratulate you when the speeding car comes by and covers you from head to toe in slush. What happens to your WOW? Maybe it turns into anger, sadness, or uncertainty. Your change in emotion will create a big change in your behavior and thus change your results for the rest of your day. You now envision a bad day ahead and feel frustrated and disappointed—and the only difference is you are now covered in slush.

In our logical world, you are led to believe that the change in your emotions, and thus in your behavior, is due to the slush. You are now completely dirty and wet, covered in slush, and it was the slush that caused you to change your behavior.

But wait, there's more to the story.

You see that speeding car turning the corner again and coming back towards you. The car stops right next to you and the driver comes rushing out. He identifies himself as the one responsible for splashing you, but he wants to explain. You let him explain even though you feel a lot of anger and frustration. He admits going too fast, but tells you that as he was driving a young boy with a knapsack was crossing the street. The only way he could avoid hitting the boy was to come closer to the sidewalk, which caused him to splash you. He apologizes. How do you feel now? Better I would think, even though you're still totally covered in slush.

NOTES _____

_____

_____

Your brain has started thinking differently because you're not as upset as you were a moment ago. Your behavior has changed as well and you start re-evaluating your day, even though you're still covered in slush.

But wait, the story's not over yet.

As the driver is about to get back into his car, he turns and asks you to look across the street to where he's pointing. He wants you to see the boy with the knapsack. You look and recognize the boy. He's your son! How do you feel now? I would think grateful, thankful, and forgiving. The slush is still all over you, but now it is totally irrelevant. Your brain is finding all kinds of solutions to your day, even though you're still totally covered in slush.

This is an extreme example and I've chosen it to illustrate the control you can have over your own emotions. If the slush had absolute power over them, then nothing would have changed your emotions until you were clean and dry. Yet you were still dirty and wet and your emotions did change, which in turn would change the whole outcome of your day. If external circumstances such as these can change your emotions, so can YOU!

Don't Let Everyday Slush Control Your Emotions

Slush only gets its power to affect our emotions from the power we give it; otherwise it can only get us dirty and wet. Slush can come in different forms and is in our lives every single day. Everyday slush can take control of our daily

NOTES

41

results if unconsciously we allow it to dictate our emotions and our behaviors.

Slush can be a comment a co-worker made about our work, a look someone gave us in the hallway, a piece of news we heard on the radio, a commercial we saw on TV, an argument we had with one of our children, a traffic jam, the weather . . . the list goes on and on. The slush that sprayed us from head to toe is an excellent example of external everyday slush, but what about the internal slush that we create inside ourselves? What do I mean by internal slush? Here are two examples that explain what I mean.

Dealing with Rejection

Joseph Ricardi, a university graduate in finance, applied for a job at a financial services firm where they sold life insurance and mutual funds. Joseph ended up getting an interview and really wanted the job. He was excited about the opportunity to become a financial advisor and build up his own practice. The interviewer explained explicitly that there was a lot of soliciting involved in the job but also explained that he would be trained to sell and that the law of averages always prevailed. This reassured Joseph and kept him excited about the job.

Joseph got the job and completed all of his training and was still enthusiastic and ready to get going. His logical side was telling him that everything would be okay because the law of averages always prevailed. However, when it came time for

NOTES

42

him to make "real" calls to real people, he started feeling nervous and feared rejection. His feelings of uncertainty intensified when Joseph worried that his prospects might not be interested in meeting him, might already have a financial advisor, or might not have time to talk with him when he called.

How did Joseph's fear of rejection influence his chances of meeting with his prospects? If Joseph made his calls feeling these emotions, the chances he would get an appointment were slim. Even if he used the telephone sales tracks he learned in training, if the prospects gave him the answer that he feared, he wouldn't persist.

Joseph needed to first tap into positive and empowering thoughts to create the proper emotions, and then use the learned sales track. He needed to tell himself that his services were needed and essential. He needed to remind himself that the prospects would like him and that it was normal for them to resist initially. Instead of focusing on the perceived rejection (the slush), Joseph needed to focus on the opportunity to meet his prospects and get to know what their needs were. He had to remember that human beings had to be sold what they *needed*, and would buy what they *wanted*.

For example, prospects often won't go out and spend $45 on a kitchen fire extinguisher (a need), but would gladly spend $3000 for a new gas or electric range (a want). Joseph needed to focus on these empowering thoughts that would create feelings of calmness, pride, and confidence, which

NOTES _____

_____

_____

would allow him to persist after the prospect's first objection. Joseph's positive emotions would reassure his prospect and create the same positive feelings in his prospect as well.

A sport analogy could be applied to Joseph's situation. Let's pretend Joseph was a great athlete and strategist who loved football. He would still have to learn "emotional fitness" and accept getting blocked or tackled or having to block and tackle if he wanted to be a successful football player.

Repetition and practice create confidence, mastery of competencies, and empowered emotions. By focusing on mastering his sales tracks, calling upon motivating thoughts to create positive emotions—in other words his controllable "I" as opposed to his self-inflicted slush—Joseph will automatically have more control over his desired results. In addition, less external slush will be attracted to him and his ratio of success per sales call will far surpass the average.

Rocking the Boat

Jason Resther was a 15-year-old going to high school and considered himself pretty much an adult. He was a good student with consistent good grades, had a 14-year-old girlfriend, played soccer on the school team, and had a good relationship with his parents. His girlfriend, Jennifer, had planned a "sweet 16" birthday party for him at her parents' house. Jason told his parents about the party and mentioned that his girlfriend wanted him to sleep over. However, Jason knew his parents' rules; they didn't want him sleeping over

NOTES

at his girlfriend's house. To make his point, he said that, after all, it was his 16th birthday; the party would end late and Jennifer's parents were okay with him staying there. Jason's parents got along well with Jason and wanted him to enjoy his 16th birthday and the party. They knew that their answer should be "*No*," but felt they should say "*Yes*" because of Jason's enthusiasm.

Jason's parents were torn between making what they believed was the appropriate decision according to their rules and not wanting to upset or disappoint Jason or his girlfriend. It's very easy to fall into the trap of saying "*Yes*" when we want to say "*No*" because we don't want to rock the boat.

Jason's parents needed to become conscious of their feelings. Their emotions were influencing their decision. By stepping out of the situation and looking in from the outside, Jason's parents could distance themselves from the uncomfortable emotions triggered by the fact that they might disappoint Jason. Stepping back created confidence and readied them for the possible negative reaction from Jason. Jason's reaction wouldn't necessarily be negative, however. He could have simply been testing the waters and not have been ready himself to sleep over, even though he asked to. It was the parents' self-inflicted slush of not wanting to rock the boat that was creating their indecision. Becoming aware of the emotions influencing their indecision helped them focus their thoughts and feelings on being responsible parents and behave according to their family values. It made them feel okay about saying "*No*," even when they might feel

NOTES

like saying *"Yes."*

There is no absolute right or wrong way to raise children, aside from what's against the law. However, saying *"Yes"* and going against one's parental values just to please is definitely not recommended. Again, we can see that by being conscious of their emotions, the consequences of their emotions, and focusing on their controllable "I," Jason's parents controlled their decision and didn't let the slush do it for them.

These two examples show us how we can inflict slush upon ourselves, creating emotions of fear, uncertainty, lack of confidence, and doubt before we're even in the situation. They clearly illustrate that internal slush doesn't help individuals achieve their desired objectives or decisions.

Taking Control

Focusing on the result we want and being conscious of our emotions, whatever they may be, is necessary to attain the outcome we desire. Thinking about different alternatives and recognizing the ones that will not help us achieve our objective is an excellent exercise. For example, you want that new job and you recognize that being self-defeating is not the best emotional state to help you attain your desired outcome. Instead, you could focus on researching the company, preparing your clothes for the interview, and believing that being prepared and professional will create the impression you want to make. Eliminating the least effective choices before we are in the situation makes the best choice

NOTES

much clearer and helps us gain confidence and a sense of control.

Focusing on your inner "I" and what your "I" can control, and not what your "I" can't control, is the key to success in any situation. This rethinking process will automatically change your emotions to more effective ones and get rid of the internal slush—those pesky emotions hindering your desired results. Taking control of your slush, before your slush controls you, is an excellent way to just do it. Begin my **DO RE ME Circle** and stop letting external and internal slush take control of your emotions. You will see astounding results as your emotions and actions are more and more in harmony with your beautiful inner "musica."

Become a Slush Buster today!

NOTES

NOTES

Chapter 5

THE
BACKWASH

Your assumptions are your window on the world. Scrub them off every once in a while, or the light won't come in.

-Alan Alda

♪ ♫
The Backwash

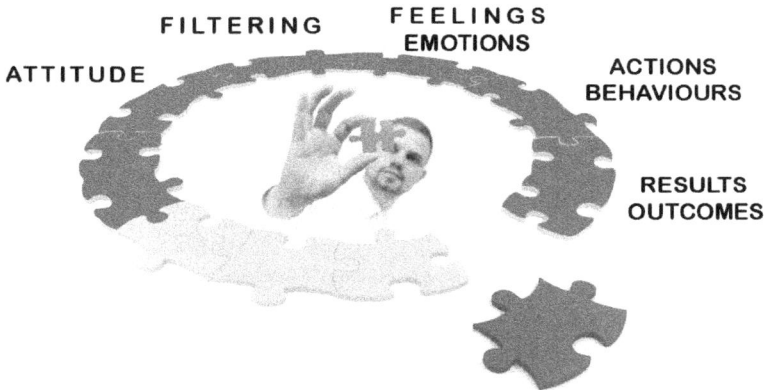

FILTERING FEELINGS
EMOTIONS

ATTITUDE

ACTIONS
BEHAVIOURS

RESULTS
OUTCOMES

It's All About Attitude

In the previous chapters, we learned how to let go and move out of the logical trap. We practiced being more aware of our emotions as a way of creating desirable behaviors and positive outcomes. We became "slush busters"!

As we continue through the DO-RE-Me Circle, we come upon one of the most important aspect of all human behavior: attitude. Attitudes dictate our emotions. They are our mental filters. They filter everything we hear, see, smell and touch.

They create an emotion in us that translates into our actions and our results. We each have our own different or unique attitude towards things. Yet we expect similar results from people with similar circumstances, talents or training. Logical, isn't it?

I mentioned in the earlier chapters that the "I" has the final word on anything we learn or are told. It is each individual's attitude that will have the last word on how we feel about something, therefore having the last word on our actions and our results. You may think that the word "attitude" is overused. People are constantly told to have a positive attitude. Unfortunately, even though we may want to, most of us don't know how to stay positive. It was never explained to us.

Cleaning Out Our Filters

Our positive attitudes are dependent on the state of our mental and emotional filters. The best way to explain how it works is by using the example of a swimming pool. Every swimming pool has a filter that filters water so the pool water stays sparkling clean. Every once in a while, we must clean this filter. We can tell by the pressure gauge whether we need to change the filter or not. When the pressure is close to the red zone, the filter needs to be cleaned. Those of you who have a pool know that this is referred to as a "backwash." When we perform a backwash, the accumulated junk is flushed out of the filter through another pipe. At the same time, the pool water

NOTES

level goes down because some of it has been used for the backwash. At the end of the backwash, we must refill the pool with clean water. We do this as often as needed to keep our pool water sparkling clean.

If I compare it to my DO-RE-ME Circle, the sparkling pool water is my desired result. The filter is my attitude. Emotions and actions are impacted by our backwash. What happens to our pool water if we don't do any backwashes? Well, the water begins to get foggy and the filter is actually working harder as indicated by the pressure gauge. Ultimately, with no backwashes, the pool water will become totally filthy and the filter will need to be replaced because it will be so clogged that it will no longer be functional.

When the "I" Gets Clogged Up

This is terrible, but not a disaster. We can go buy a new filter and replace the old one. When it comes to human beings however, it is much more serious. Not performing our mental backwashes where we get rid of the "junk" in our attitudes so it can be replaced with beautiful and new exciting thoughts will end up with us burning out or getting depressed. This happens unconsciously. We are not getting the results we want and all we have ever been taught is to work harder. So we work harder with a dirty filter and continue to do so to get the results until our body gives up. Of course, not everyone will suffer a burnout or depression if they don't do their backwashes. However, we are putting ourselves in a position where we need

NOTES

to work harder to get the same results and sometimes even less than desired results. Over the years we can build up plenty of junk in our mental filter. Most of us don't burnout, but we do suffer from a decrease in enthusiasm, in passion, in the love of our jobs or in our relationships.

Why is it that so many teachers who have been teaching for over 20 years don't have the same spark or enthusiasm they once did? I'm sure that if we asked them if one of their objectives for the day was to teach with LESS enthusiasm they would answer "*No.*" Yet, that's exactly what they do. Of course, one of the factors may be age and routine, but it doesn't necessarily have to be so. The number one factor for their lack of enthusiasm is a combination of them being in an "unconscious incompetence" state, not having done any backwashes in a long time and not nourishing their attitude with beautiful and powerful thoughts. More often than not, were you to ask the teachers if their objective was to teach with less enthusiasm, that question alone would bring their awareness from an unconscious state (unconscious incompetence) to a conscious one (conscious incompetence) and allow a backwash to begin.

This example is not unique to the teaching profession. It happens to everyone. We all get clogged up every once in a while. Do you think that the loss of passion and romance in a relationship is planned? I believe you would say "*No.*" Why does it happen so often then? The answer: no backwashes, no replenishing and no specific action. We allow ourselves to drift into "unconscious incompetence" and the effort to filter

NOTES

the accumulated junk is so large that we have no energy left for passion or romance. We easily accept the importance of exercise and good food for a healthy body. What about a healthy mind, heart and soul? I believe that they are just as important, if not more so.

Getting Rid of the Junk

Can you imagine not being allowed to take out the garbage for three to four weeks on your street? You would be forced to keep it inside your house somewhere. After the first week, you would need to tend to the bad odor that's spreading in your home. Since you are now tending to this extra new task, it takes away time from more pleasant ones. Week two goes by and it's only getting worse because the first week's garbage is creating more problems. Week three and then week four go by . . . Do I need to outline the major problem? In addition to dealing with the odor and hygiene, you now have a space issue. The garbage is starting to take up more and more space and you have less and less room for pleasant items. Look at all that effort that is being wasted just to take care of the garbage. All this because you didn't take one simple weekly action: taking out the garbage. Imagine decades of this! Well, this is what happens when we don't take the time to filter and clear out our emotional, mental and attitudinal junk.

The beauty and problem of human beings is that we are resilient. Beauty, because we can overcome practically

NOTES

anything. Problem, because sometimes it takes a long time before we become aware of the issues. In the same way that pressure goes down on the pool filter after a backwash while keeping the pool water sparkling clean, I guarantee you that by doing your own inner backwashes regularly, you will find yourself re-energized and able to use less effort to achieve the same or even superior results.

Time for a Backwash

How about a backwash right now? You'll feel great! Think of something that is causing you grief, pain, stress, sadness, anxiety or some other unpleasant emotion. It could be related to your work or your personal life.

For example, you may think you will never be able to get through all the follow-ups at work, or that the presentation you need to do won't be good, or that your prospective client will not buy your product, or that your son or daughter won't finish university, or that you will not get the promotion that you applied for, or that you will not be able to learn the new software for your job, or that your spouse is no longer interested in you.

Identify and write down the unpleasant thoughts. Now that you have written them down, it's time to do your backwash. Let them go, wash and filter them out and replace them with opposite positive thoughts. Continue to constantly and consciously repeat them to yourself so that the old thoughts don't come back. Remember, the old thoughts (unconscious

NOTES _____

_____

_____

incompetence) want to come back, so you will need to remain conscious of that until your new thoughts have permanently replaced the old ones.

Once this is done, choose ONE specific action that will help you to achieve your objective. Remember, if you choose that action without first doing the backwash it won't work because the old thoughts will creep up on you and impact the results of your action.

For example, to this day, I still get anxious and uncertain about a speech or presentation that I need to make. I identify those thoughts and replace them with positive ones. For example, I tap into my desire to make a difference or I think about a warm grateful note I received after a speech. I then go ahead with my ONE specific action, which is to review everything that "I" can and practice until I feel totally confident, knowing full well that I cannot control everything.

How do athletes compete when they need to compete against someone who is, according to statistics and logic, far superior to them? They backwash and replenish with positive thoughts and concentrate on ONE specific action. Interestingly, the same holds true for the athlete who is "statistically" favored. She backwashes and replenishes, then performs one specific action.

There are many wonderful techniques and approaches that you can use to do your backwash. I encourage you to explore and use what works for you. Depending on how much cleansing you need to do, you may even decide to work with a coach or counselor.

NOTES _____

_____

_____

Turn up your "musica," start cleaning, be creative and take charge of your attitude today! The backwashes will replenish you with passion, energy and overall pleasure.

NOTES

Chapter 6

WE ARE
WHAT
WE BELIEVE

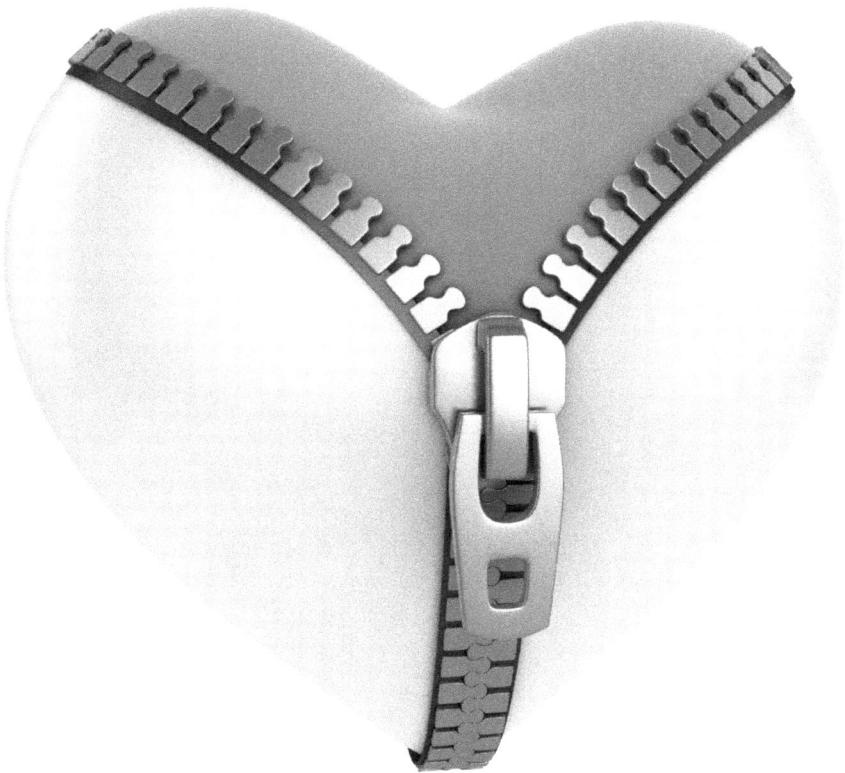

"Choose beliefs that serve your soul—choose beliefs that serve the grander dream of who you choose to be."

- Joy Page

♪ ♫

We Are
What We Believe

It's All About Beliefs

We're almost at the end of our DO-RE-ME Circle. We've just finished our "backwash" and we have replaced our negative thoughts with new positive thinking which in turn can generate more empowering beliefs. This process is important because it is our beliefs that create our attitudes. We need to remember that since we don't all have the same beliefs, we cannot expect the same behavior from everybody based on the fact that they come from the same background or training. We also need to remember when we base our expectations uniquely on logic, we stand to be disappointed.

If we listen carefully to people, we will discover their beliefs. We are all what we believe. When was the last time you listened to yourself? You would be surprised what you would discover about yourself. Our beliefs will always have the last word. They dictate our attitudes which in turn dictate our emotions which trigger our actions which in turn determine our results. This is happening constantly at speeds that we cannot even notice. If we don't make an effort to become aware of our beliefs (conscious competence) then it will be practically impossible to change our behavior to impact our results.

We may want to take a course on time management because we believe we're not good time managers. The course will have little or no impact if we don't change our belief about our ability to be good time managers. When we alter our beliefs, we automatically give our brain the command to change in order to live up to those new beliefs. Our brain will automatically start looking for things to do that match our beliefs.

However, if a person's beliefs haven't changed, chances are the behaviors won't either. This is one of the primary reasons why companies spend fortunes on training and don't ever get the expected results. Those great training binders will just continue to collect dust and so will the new documents that will replace them.

NOTES

62

Remember the advertising industry I told you about in the earlier chapters? Advertisers know they are at their best when they create a belief in us that lasts. It's called branding. This is when just the sight or mention of a brand creates positive emotions in us about the product. That's what slogans are for too. A slogan is just a marketing term for a belief. Coke is the "Real Thing," Pepsi is the "New Generation," Clairol says "Blondes have more fun," Michelin says that "A lot more is riding on your tires," and BMW is the "Ultimate Driving Machine."

Why do wars still happen today? Where does racism come from? Why do battered women allow themselves to continue to be beaten? What is every religion based on? What makes you do what you do? The answer to all these questions is the same. It's your beliefs.

A few years ago, when I was at the hospital with my Mom at the oncology department, I overheard a discussion about battered women. One lady suggested that if women would just leave their husbands alone when they became verbally abusive, then they wouldn't be beaten. Although to most of us this may seem absurd, it was totally reasonable for this lady. That is what she believed.

The Power of Beliefs

I mentioned at the beginning of my book that for two years I taught students with learning difficulties. I began teaching in October of the first year instead of September since three

NOTES

other teachers had started before me. Two of them quit after a month and the other was asked to leave. The class average was 55 and I was to teach English as a second language to French speaking students. Up to then, the students had been taught through a "logical" approach.

All teachers want their students to succeed but teaching in a logical way will not always get the desired results. How do "logical" teachers teach? Well, they will explain the material and if the students don't understand, they will repeat it. If the students still don't understand they will repeat it a second time. However, if a third explanation is necessary, this will reinforce their logical belief regarding the students' limited ability to learn and will influence how they "look" at them. Logically, three explanations are more than enough. If the students still don't understand, well then it's just too bad. The problem with this kind of belief is that it becomes a self-fulfilling prophecy. If the students' beliefs about themselves don't change, then there isn't much hope. Studies tend to point out that just the "look" a teacher has towards the students has a bigger influence on learning than all the explanations they can give on the subject matter. This, I am sure, also applies to anyone who wants to bring out the best in people and help them grow.

Since I was not a "logical" teacher, I knew that to affect change in the student's results, I needed to help them change their beliefs. They believed that they were not smart and that their class average of 55 was normal. I created two rules in the classroom. The first rule was when I asked them a question they could give me any answer they wanted except "*je ne sais pas*," which means "*I don't know*" in English. The second rule was when I asked them to do workbook exercises in class they were allowed to ask me for explanations as many times as they wished, but were not allowed to say "*je ne suis pas capable*," which means "*I can't do it*" in English.

I chose these rules because they would have a direct and immediate impact on their beliefs. So as I asked my first question in that first month to one of the students, she answered, "*je ne sais pas*." This didn't upset me at all. Only a logical teacher would have responded "*Didn't I tell you not to say that?*" which of course would have made things worse.

In fact, I expected it. The student was in logical mode and since she truly didn't know the answer, that's all she could say. I also knew that the student didn't know, but my objective was not to see who knew the answer. My goal was to create new beliefs in all the students so that ultimately their results would improve. When that student answered "*je ne sais pas*," I knew I needed to do a mini «backwash» on the spot and replace her current beliefs with new positive beliefs. I looked at her straight in the eyes and with confidence told her that yes, she *did* know and I invited her to just give it a try. She insisted that she didn't know. Another mini «backwash» was needed. So, with a positive "look," I repeated that she *did* know the answer and to give it a try. It was only on the fourth attempt that the student answered, only to get rid of me.

Another reason why the students didn't want to risk answering was because they were already convinced they had the wrong answer. They were also afraid they would get the same kind of feedback they were used to receiving from logical teachers, which resulted in making them feel "not too smart." So when this first student finally risked an answer, she was expecting to hear "*You're wrong.*" Instead and even though her answer wasn't right, I said "you almost got it" with a very positive and confident "look" towards her.

For the first time in their life, these students were told that they "almost got it" even though it was the wrong answer. At least for that moment, they believed they weren't that bad. I went on to another student with the same positive "look" and attitude. At first, he also responded "*je ne sais pas,*" but only twice. He had seen how it went with the other student. His answer was also wrong, and I responded, "*Oh, we almost got it.*"

You see, everyone was contributing to the right answer even with wrong answers. I always made sure that I would get the right answer from one of the students even if I had to give them the answer one letter at a time. So when a student would finally give the right answer I would say, "*Bravo! We got it!*" WE GOT IT, what a special statement!

Over the following months, I was able to help the students believe in themselves, which resulted in more and more right answers from everyone. I had helped them do their "backwashes" without them knowing what was happening. All they knew was that for some reason it was getting easier and easier to study and to get the right answers. The class average at the end of the year was 72. Wow! I hadn't changed

NOTES

the curriculum or the students. However, their beliefs about themselves had changed and therefore so did their results. They were still who they believed they were, except their beliefs were now different.

Choosing Empowering Beliefs

How do we explain why employees all of a sudden feel they cannot do their job? Have they forgotten everything overnight? Have they become incompetent? No, something has influenced and changed their beliefs. Do a "backwash" with them, find out what has changed their beliefs and replenish them with positive, empowering beliefs.

This approach has served me well throughout my life. Back when I was heading my own financial services agency, I remember one particularly challenging time. The industry was going through major changes which would require increased responsibilities and new competencies from our staff. We had a management meeting to address these and other issues with the team. When it came to discussing these inevitable changes, the manager responsible for the staff shared that there was a huge problem. The solution, according to him, could not be found within the present staff. He reported that they felt stressed, helpless and incompetent in the face of these changes and he didn't think it would be possible to get them to acquire new competencies or assume more responsibility.

I told the manager that before any decisions were made

NOTES

regarding staffing, I wanted him to go home that evening and think. I challenged him to reflect on whether or not he believed in his staff. We agreed to meet the following morning. When we met the next day, I could sense a change in his attitude. He told me that he had taken the time to think about this very deeply and had come to the conclusion that he believed wholeheartedly in his staff. He also felt good about himself and in his capacity to lead them through this important transition. As a result, he had already figured out what to do with each individual and how it would all work out. All this because his beliefs towards his team had changed. Results were amazing.

Believing in yourself and believing in other people can make a big difference. Have you noticed that one of the most common statements made when someone is accepting an award, such as an Oscar, Grammy, Peoples' Choice Award, or American Music Award, is *"Thank you for believing in me!"*

Making Beliefs Work for You

When was the last time you checked what your beliefs were? What beliefs are stopping you from achieving what you want to achieve? From feeling the way you want to feel? Are you being stifled by limiting beliefs such as: I'm too old, I'm too young, nothing will change, that's the way it's always been, I'm not good at this, it will never work, there's never enough time, I can never get organized . . . The list can go on and on. What if the opposite was true? What if you decided to tune

NOTES

In to a different song? The time may be ripe for another "backwash."

No matter how good we may be, our beliefs have the last and most important say. Don't let others decide for you. Decide and choose your own beliefs. Dance to the beat of your own "musica"!

NOTES _____

NOTES

Chapter 7

PROGRAMMING

"A goal without a plan is just a wish."

-Antoine de Saint-Exupéry

♪ ♫
Programming

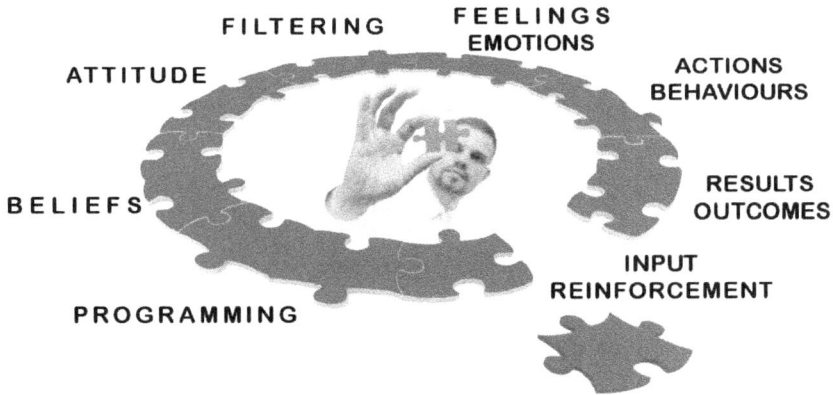

FILTERING FEELINGS EMOTIONS

ATTITUDE ACTIONS BEHAVIOURS

BELIEFS RESULTS OUTCOMES

INPUT REINFORCEMENT

PROGRAMMING

It's All In the Programming

We are now at the end of the DO-RE-Me Circle. We started with results, then actions, emotions, attitude and beliefs. Let's move on to programming. I started our journey referring to our computers and walking our talk. Just like our computer, our brain which is the most complex and powerful computer around, will function according to the way it has been programmed. Do we really know what our programming is?

My guess is no, not really. Some of us are more conscious than others, but we can all improve.

As you saw in my earlier chapters, we must put ourselves in a state of consciousness if we want to change or improve. The same applies to programming. We must be in a conscious mode to be able to identify our programming before we can replace it. This is a challenge but worth every effort. You see, regardless of our current programming, if we are not conscious of how we're being or have been programmed, we will only continue to reinforce the existing and sometimes deficient programs. I call this the boomerang effect. We reap what we sow. I've illustrated this in the DO-RE-ME Circle through reinforcement. Sow good seeds (positive input), nurture the plant with healthy elements (positive reinforcement) and positive programming will take place. The opposite is also true.

Choosing a Conscious State of Mind

Since our tendency is to stay in our comfort zone, we will unconsciously be drawn to programming that's similar to our existing programs. By remaining in our unconscious state without doing any backwashes, we will only continue to reinforce our current behavior and therefore keep getting the same results. Unfortunately, most people will only change their programming if they're forced to do so by external circumstances such as the loss of a loved one, a divorce, the loss of a job, the birth of a child or an illness. I strongly encourage you not to wait for some outside force before starting to

NOTES

74

question your internal unconscious programming.

Our programming began at birth and some studies even suggest it could have started during our time in the womb. This means that most of our programming happened when we were not even in a position to choose it, let alone realize that we were being programmed. Throughout our school years and beyond, we acquired loads of knowledge. Very little of it, however, was about what makes us who we are. Ask yourself these questions:

♪   What makes me happy, and why?

♪   What do I like or not like about my job, and why?

♪   How often do I take the time to compliment someone, and why?

♪   When was the last time I sent someone a handwritten note just to wish them well, and why?

♪   When was the last time I told my son or daughter, or husband or wife, or father or mother, or friend, that I was proud of them, and why?

♪   When was the last time I gave thanks for my job, my health, my pleasure, and why?

NOTES

I'm sure you get my point. The answer to all the whys, by the way, is the same. It's because of our programming. If we don't consciously choose our programming, we automatically leave it up to others to choose it for us. Who are those "others"? They could be your uncle, your father, your boss, your colleagues, TV, radio, newspapers, magazines, movies, your husband, your wife or advertising. Everyone and everything but you. Everyone and everything but the "I."

My hope is that you take responsibility for your own programming and free yourself from negative programming. Bring in new positive notes to your sound track and start composing your new and improved DO-RE-ME Circle. You will feel more satisfaction and more happiness as you start reaping new and improved results in all aspects of your life!

Here are two very simple examples of what I believe to be unconscious programming that you have allowed yourself to accept. One example is from your professional life and the other concerns your personal life. You will see how you can change that programming to bring about a new sense of perspective and generate better results.

How Irresistible is Your Voice Mail?

The first example is about your voice mail. We all have voice mail at work. And yes, some of us still use it! The important question is: how do we use it? Unconsciously, we view it strictly as a tool for people to leave a message. I want to challenge you: it is much more than that. It is your personal

NOTES

advertising, representing who you are and properly done can be a formidable tool to offer great service, leave a lasting positive feeling with your callers and be a great timesaver and organizer.

However, this is not the case for most people. Let me guess what your voice mail probably sounds like, *"Hello, you have reached . . . , I am not available right now, but please leave me a message, and I will call you back as soon as possible."* Am I pretty close to what your message sounds like? I'm pretty sure I am.

This is a perfect example of action triggered by unconscious programming. In addition, we don't realize that this type of voice mail message is not extremely effective. It is LOGICAL, however. First of all, it's far from different or creative because it sounds like a million other voice mail messages. And, what does "as soon as possible" mean?

At this stage, you may be saying, *"Come on Giovanni, it means as soon as possible."* My response is, *"Okay, and when is that?"* The real answer is: it could be in one hour, two hours, tomorrow, in 15 minutes, in two days . . . who knows. Here's the problem. Each caller has his and her own definition of what "as soon as possible" means and it will be impossible to satisfy all the callers according to their own definitions.

So now, you have guaranteed that you will NOT satisfy all the callers, which is exactly the opposite of what you want to achieve. Why do we say "as soon as possible"? First of all, we have not taken the time to consciously design an efficient and original message. Secondly, "as soon as possible" sounds

NOTES _____

_____

_____

fantastic when in fact it is subjective and relative. Lastly, this is what's been said for many, many years and we just repeat it since we've been programmed to say it. We have put ourselves in a situation where we will constantly be interrupting our work to return messages because we have programmed our brain to call people back as soon as we can.

Let me give you an example of what my voice mail sounds like, "*Hello, this is Giovanni Gaudelli. If you leave me a message before 4:30 pm today, I guarantee I will call you back before 5 pm, and if not before 9 am on our next working day. Thank you and have a wonderfully, effervescent day!*" I have used the key items in the DO-RE-ME Circle. I "program" my caller with a specific expectation and leave them with a positive emotion. The keys to a compelling voice mail message are as follows:

♪   Say your name with pride.

♪   Be specific about your promises.

♪   Use the word guarantee (people just love it).

♪   Finish with a WOW enthusiastic original wish.

I can already feel your old programming putting up a fight. This is normal because I am bringing you into a conscious

NOTES

incompetent state, which is very uncomfortable. That is why I have provided you with an example of a conscious competent model. I am convinced that you can create your own excellent message and begin receiving the enormous benefits from it. Just follow the steps I showed you. The results for you will be many:

♪ No more rushing to call all people back right away.

♪ You will feel less stressed and more in control.

♪ You'll be calling people back according to a specific schedule that you've set.

♪ By sorting out which messages need immediate attention from those that can wait, you will be able to deal with priorities calmly and more efficiently.

Imagine you set up an appointment with someone next week and the time of the appointment is "as soon as possible." How will you schedule that in? To respect that appointment you will have to be free when that occurs and how do you know when that will be for sure? By being specific, you can now deal with your call backs in an organized way without constantly interrupting your work to do so. More importantly, you will have happy, satisfied callers who, believe me, will return

NOTES

the WOW greeting to you by wishing you the same.

One last comment about your voice mail message: if your callers are mostly elders, then it is even more important not to say "as soon as possible" because they will literally wait next to the phone all day for your call. They will even interrupt their telephone conversations with their relatives or friends because they are waiting for your call and don't want to miss it. If they miss your call, they have "no guarantee" when you will call back again. Imagine, if you don't call them back before the end of the day, they go to bed not knowing if you'll call back tomorrow. All this because of "as soon as possible" that could have been successfully replaced by a more specific guarantee.

Ever ordered a pizza and wanted to know when you would receive it? Do you prefer they tell you "as soon as possible" and you just wait and hope, or that they guarantee within the next 45 minutes?

I have used this example to illustrate how programming can impact our results. Something as simple as our voice mail with a logical message of "as soon as possible" can impede our results, create unnecessary stress and demand additional efforts on our part. By being more conscious of external programming and choosing to re-program ourselves, we can do wonders with our lives.

Like anything, it will take conscious effort at the beginning, but it will become easier and easier as time goes by and as you become more in control of your programming. Remember that brushing your teeth also started the same way.

NOTES

What's In a Day?

The second example I want to share with you is the TGIF phenomenon: the "Thank God It's Friday" phenomenon. Everyone is feeling great, smiles are abundant and energy is fantastic. Yet most people have chores waiting for them at home, such as raking the leaves, painting the garage floor, fixing the roof, doing laundry, buying groceries, driving the kids to hockey practice at 5:00 am on Saturday morning and so on.

Regardless of the chores waiting for us, we love Fridays. However, when Monday comes around and we're asked how we're feeling, the response sounds something like this, "Well, not so bad for a Monday. I was so busy on the weekend; I didn't have time to stop. I'm so tired." Yet, I'm sure they can't wait for the next weekend for a repeat of the same . . . all over again.

You see, the reason why Fridays are so great is because we've been programmed to believe that they are. Therefore, no matter what happens on a Friday, it's always okay. TGIF has become one of our beliefs as a result of the constant programming coming from everywhere, including radio, TV, our work or our friends. I want to challenge you to re-program yourself and create a new belief so that everyday can be fantastic, not just Fridays.

There are seven days in a week and Fridays are only one-seventh of your life. How many days of your life do you want to be just like Fridays? I'm sure you wouldn't want only one. Hopefully you said seven. Well the good news is that you

NOTES

can now do something about it and no one can stop you. Why? Because you can choose to re-program yourself.

You can decide that every day, even Monday, is great. I guarantee you that by re-programming yourself to make every day spectacular you will put in motion a vivacious positive cycle making your life outstanding. In addition, one of the side effects will be that "slush" will stay away from you all week, in the same way it stays away from you on Friday. Wouldn't that be fantastic? You are on your way to making every day of the week absolutely fabulous. Although you may never fully achieve making every day totally awesome, you will surely end up enjoying more amazing days than if you didn't change your programming.

Remember that you are constantly assailed with programming whether you like it or not. So, start being conscious of it and take charge of your own programming. If you do, you will take charge of your beliefs, your attitudes, your emotions, your actions and your results. Create your own special "musica." Create your own positive, motivating DO-RE-ME Circle. Remember: What goes around comes around.

NOTES _____

_____

_____

_____

_____

_____

Chapter 7 ♫ PROGRAMMING

NOTES

Chapter 8

LA MUSICA

I hope when you count the stars you begin with yourself. And may you embrace the moonlight with your dreams.

-Dodinsky

♪ ♫
La Musica

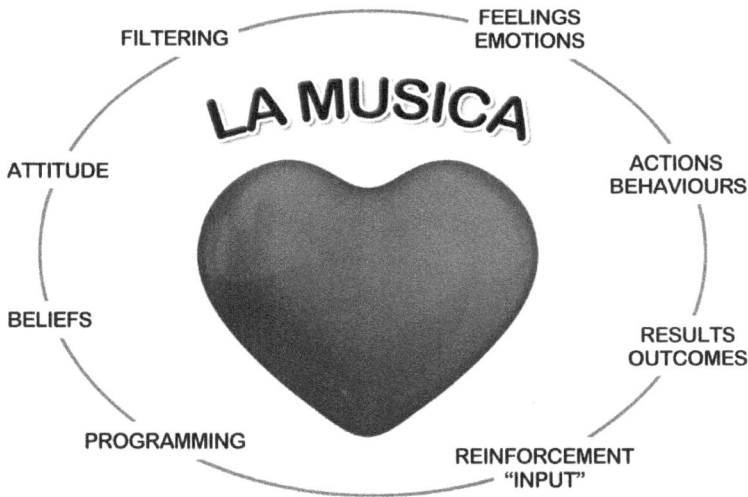

The Power of Music

I have included a heart inside the DO-RE-ME Circle, which I call "La Musica." This is the music that plays within us all the time, even though we are not always conscious of it. I'm sure you know how powerful music can be. It's even used with chemotherapy patients for its soothing effect. Patients very often bring their favorite music to listen to while they receive their treatment. Listening to music makes them feel better and this can contribute positively to the outcome of the treatment. Ancient cultures have been using music for centuries to actually heal people.

Today, rock bands fill stadiums because people want to hear them play their music. People will pay ridiculous prices to go hear their favorite artists. Even though most hockey, basketball, baseball or tennis games can be viewed on TV in the comfort of our homes, lots of people pay very high prices for tickets to see the games live. Why? Fans prefer the live ambiance, the music and the roar of the crowd. All this makes them feel great and at least for a while, it has a positive impact on their behavior and experience. Our "musica" is energy, and energy is contagious and powerful.

What would movies be like without background music? Just the music itself can make a scene feel more suspenseful, passionate, sad, exciting or funny. Even when movies had no soundtracks, there was a piano player in the theatre creating moods and feelings for the different scenes. We can recall the music from "Peter and the Wolf" that translates remarkably well the characters and all the action. We can remember Vivaldi's "Four Seasons" whose harmonies evoke the passage of the different seasons and their influence on our emotional state.

The Music Within

Imagine how important it is to be playing the appropriate

NOTES

music inside of you when communicating with your children, your spouse, your parents, your colleagues, your staff and your superiors. I said at the beginning of my book that we are ALL in our own way leaders. It is that music within us that makes the difference between a good leader and a great one. Great leaders realize the importance of recognizing the music within the people they're leading. Great leaders know that this music is a result of beliefs and it is totally essential for understanding the reasons behind people's behavior. This helps great leaders demonstrate empathy and caring towards people.

Our internal music is so very powerful. Our internal music will always speak louder than our words. No matter what we say, the power of our message will be measured much more by our internal music than our words. Songs with great lyrics and bad music don't have much impact. Great music with so-so lyrics works very well. And of course great music with great lyrics is WOW!

Opera is a perfect example. Most people are moved by powerful arias even though they probably don't understand any of the words. Children communicate through "their own music" in the early months of their life before they can speak. They respond to all types of music irrelevant of language. This extraordinary capacity remains with us but we unconsciously lose touch with it as we grow older, become more logical, accumulate more junk in our filters and are too busy just going through the motions of living. However, if you choose to remain conscious and program or re-program yourself every

NOTES

day, you will awaken and re-create that beautiful music within. You will feel energized and will energize others around you through your internal music.

It will show in your smile, in the way you walk, look at others, drive, cook, make love, shake hands, hug . . . everything will be better. The beauty, as mentioned earlier, is what goes around comes around, so all this magnificent music will also come back to you.

Scientists are now studying the effect of music on human beings. They are able to see the significant effects different types of music have on our neurological system. So much so, that they are experimenting with treatments based on playing certain kinds of music. Scientists have also observed the power of music on Alzheimer's patients. For some reason they can forget almost everything, but recognize a song and even sing it. In some cases, researchers have even seen some of the symptoms of Alzheimer's decrease. They may no longer recognize their loved ones, but can still recognize their internal music.

Start Playing Your Song

We are all capable of having outstanding music playing within us. However, if we do not choose our programming it will be chosen for us and our internal music will be chosen for us too. Remember in chapter 6, I mention that the "look" teachers have towards their students has a tremendous impact on their beliefs and learning. That "look" is really an

NOTES _____

_____

_____

expression of their internal music. Just like your iPod or CD player, you can choose what is playing inside of you. It's a question of how you want to program yourself.

So please, don't allow your internal music to become off-key. From now on, program yourself every day with inspiring thoughts and don't allow external negative programming to influence you. Your programming, your DO-RE-ME Circle, will begin to create new positive beliefs. Your beliefs will create your attitude towards everything around you, and so affect your emotions and influence your results. This will automatically create that inspiring "musica" inside of you, which will also inspire all those around you.

Remember, it is not your words that can best express how you feel; it's your internal "musica"! So, start playing your song!

NOTES

Chapter 9

31.5 SIMPLE REPROGRAMMING IDEAS

The person who says it cannot be done should not interrupt the person who is doing it.

-Chinese Proverb

♪ ♫

31.5 Simple
Reprogramming Ideas

Small Things Make a Big Difference

I have taken you on a journey, a pleasant one I hope, where I have challenged you to become more conscious and take control of your beliefs. My sincere hope is that, as a result, I have helped you in a simple way to find the leader within. I hope that you are well on your way to becoming your own maestro, sharing your beautiful "musica" and making every part of your life better.

To keep you going, I am providing you with 31.5 examples of re-programming to help you take control of your own programming. You will notice that they are simple and will help you get out of your comfort zone.

Why 31.5?

I chose to share 31 ideas, one for each day of the longest month and invite you to complete the half idea (0.5). I also encourage you to keep adding to the list by creating some ideas of your own.

I strongly believe in the tremendous power of the "musica" within all of you. So, start playing your song and let your "musica" be heard!

31.5 Simple Reprogramming Ideas:

1. Next time you ask for a wake-up call, ask to be called 3 minutes before the hour or 3 minutes after the hour. For example, instead of 7:00 am ask for 6:57 am or 7:03 am. Those 3 little minutes will allow you to step out of your routine and remain "consciously creative."

2. Zest up your day! Ask for lemon zest with your espresso. Everyone will remember you.

3. If you're receiving great service at a restaurant, ask to speak to the manager to express your gratitude regarding the wonderful experience created by the person who is serving you. You will make two people very happy.

4. Bring a gift to your loved ones on a Tuesday and just say it's just because it's Tuesday and you love them. Everyone loves a nice surprise.

NOTES _____

_____

_____

5. Take note of people's names wherever you are and address them by their name. You'll see, it's very WOW!

6. Give someone a tip in a restaurant before she has even served you. This will put her in a very cheerful and hospitable mindset.

7. Leave a very positive compliment on someone's voice mail after working hours. Not only will that make that person's next day start beautifully, but the compliment will certainly be remembered the next time you have a conversation.

8. Tell your children or parents that you're proud of them. It's the least you can do and all this love will multiply and come back to you.

9. If you're stuck in traffic, call a few people to give them a compliment. This will not only make their day but also put you in a good mood.

10. On Mondays, find a way to make your day begin on a great note. It will make the rest of the week equally great.

11. Send a pizza to your child's teacher. She may be surprised but it will put a smile on her face.

NOTES

12. Every day congratulate yourself and be thankful for what you have. It will remind you that some people may not be as fortunate.

13. Help an elder today. Someday you will be one.

14. Write a poem. It might not change the world but it could change you.

15. Guys, get a shave from your barber. Not only will you get a great shave, but you will have treated yourself to a relaxing moment.

16. When walking by a homeless person give them a smile too. You will add tremendous value to the money or food you have shared.

17. Next time you're in the elevator, stop off at a different floor than yours. Walk around and observe. To discover new perspectives, we need to change our point of view.

18. Take a different route to work today. Taking the road less travelled can bring us to wonderful discoveries.

19. Take a different route back home from work today. More wonderful discoveries are waiting for you.

NOTES _____

_____

_____

20. Bake or buy a cake and celebrate the day. Every day is a holiday.

21. Pick a phone number randomly and when you're told it's the wrong number, wish the person a spectacular day. Making somebody's day can also make yours shine.

22. Go for a walk in the rain. For once in your life, you can pretend you're Gene Kelly.

23. Offer to wash your neighbor's car. This will probably be returned to you on a day when you really don't feel like washing yours.

24. Remember that your mother is also your spouse's mother-in-law. It will change your perception of your mother-in-law.

25. Try olive oil on your toast. This is more original than butter, jam or peanut butter and it will remind you to add some fantasy in your life.

26. Always add a sprinkle of grace to everything you do. Honey is more attractive than vinegar.

27. Be different and not indifferent. Other people will be less indifferent to your uniqueness.

NOTES

28. Once a day, close your eyes and remember the beauty that's around you. When you open your eyes, you will be more aware of the beauty in your surroundings.

29. Buy a book for someone today. Small gifts nurture friendships.

30. Have a Thanksgiving meal this month and every month. Small pleasures inspire great deeds. It will also remind you to be grateful for everything that you have.

31. The rest of your life starts today. How will you start it? Reach for those great goals, because you can!

31.5 Today, I will...

I'm sure by now you have caught on to this and are becoming great at creating new ideas!

I hug you with all my "musica"! Enjoy your new life!

NOTES

NOTES

NOTES

"You can go as far as your mind lets you. What you believe, remember you can achieve.

-Mary Kay Ash

ABOUT GIOVANNI GAUDELLI

Giovanni Gaudelli, B.A., DipEd.
Motivational & Keynote Speaker,
Coach, and Consultant

Giovanni Gaudelli is one of North America's most dynamic motivational and keynote speakers. He speaks English, French and Italian fluently, giving conferences in all three languages. For more than 15 years, this accomplished and outstanding speaker has engaged and uplifted audiences by delivering his presentations with passion, humor and authenticity. Giovanni understands that people are the heart and soul of every organization and relationship. Whether he's speaking to executives, managers, sales teams, customer service or support staff, his unique conference style creates a memorable, positive impact that lasts. People from all walks of life have changed their outlook after hearing Giovanni's message.

In his book *La Musica – Are You Playing Your Song?*, Giovanni shares his uplifting message by taking the readers on a self-discovery journey and leads them to tune in to their own beautiful harmony. He sheds an empowering light on people's abilities to become the best they can be so they can obtain better and more satisfying results in all aspects of their lives.

Giovanni graduated with a B.A. in English Literature and Italian as a Second Language and a Diploma in Education from McGill University in Montreal, Canada. He began his career teaching high school English where his enthusiasm and dynamic approach boosted the students' self-esteem and remarkably increased their ability to learn.

In 1980, wanting a new challenge, Giovanni started working with the London Life Insurance Company. As an insurance representative, he received the "Recruit of the Year" title followed by the "Chartered Life Underwriter" title, and for every year in his position, the «Million Dollar Round Table» title. Four years later, he was promoted to assistant-manager. His leadership and coaching techniques motivated average sales teams to achieve excellence and he quickly became extremely successful in the financial services industry. He went on to manage a London Life regional center. Under his leadership, the center substantially increased its performance and became the "model" financial center in terms of recruiting, training and management.

From 1998 to 2010, Giovanni directed and owned an SFL-Desjardins Financial Security franchise. He acquired the financial center during the merger of the Laurentian Life Insurance Group with Desjardins and rose to the challenge of integrating both cultures. With indomitable courage, passion, and dedication, he rebuilt the company from the ground up by setting up a caring and dynamic recruiting, training and management culture with a keen focus on people's ability to learn and grow. He maintained superior personnel retention and enviable company performance up to the sale of his franchise in 2010.

In the late 1990s, Giovanni started sharing his ideas and unique personal development approach through speaking engagements. Since the sale of his business, he devotes his energy and creative vision to his speaking, consulting and coaching engagements, helping people develop winning attitudes and beliefs that support them in achieving their goals.

Learn More About Giovanni Gaudelli's Inspiring Work:

GiovanniGaudelli.com

Twitter: @giomotivation

♪♫♪

Splendor Publishing

Splendor Publishing's life-changing books are written by skilled and passionate leaders, entrepreneurs, and experts with a mission to make a positive impact in the lives of others.

Splendor books inspire and encourage personal, professional, and spiritual growth. For information about our book titles, authors, or publishing process, or for wholesale ordering for conferences, seminars, events, or training, visit SplendorPublishing.com.